EASY CLASSICS

FOR THE YOUNG CLARINET PLAYER

T0056304

CURNOW®
MUSIC

Exclusively Distributed By

HAL•LEONARD®
CORPORATION

7777 W. BLUEMOUND RD. P.O. BOX 13819 MILWAUKEE, WI 53213

Order Number: CMP 1059-05-400

EASY CLASSICS FOR THE YOUNG CLARINET PLAYER
Clarinet

ISBN 90-431-2379-X

CD number: 19-074-3 CMP

FOR THE YOUNG CLARINET PLAYER

FOREWORD

EASY CLASSICS FOR THE YOUNG CLARINET PLAYER is a compilation of solo/recital material from the great masters of musical composition that have been specifically arranged for the Beginner through Early Intermediate instrumental soloist. The soloist will find a wide variety of styles and varying levels of difficulty in this book.

This set includes the Piano accompaniment, the Solo part, and a professionally recorded CD that demonstrates each piece. Use these examples to help develop proper performance practices. There is also a recording of the accompaniment alone that can be used for performance (and rehearsal) when a live accompaniment is not available.

EASY CLASSICS

FOR THE YOUNG CLARINET PLAYER

CONTENTS

Track   page

1   **Tuning Note C**

2 **3**   **1. ODE TO JOY** 6
Ludwig van Beethoven, *arranged by Timothy Johnson*

4 **5**   **2. SANCTUS** 9
Franz Schubert, *arranged by James Curnow*

6 **7**   **3. DAGGER DANCE from "NATOMA"** 13
Victor Herbert, *arranged by Craig Alan*

8 **9**   **4. FINALE FROM SYMPHONY No. 1** 16
Johannes Brahms, *arranged by Timothy Johnson*

10 **11**   **5. FANTAISIE IMPROMPTU** 20
Frederic Chopin, *arranged by Ann Lindsay*

12 **13**   **6. HUNGARIAN DANCE No.6** 22
Johannes Brahms, *arranged by Ann Lindsay*

14 **15**   **7. WALTZ** 26
Johannes Brahms, *arranged by James Curnow*

16 **17**   **8. ANDANTE from LA CI DAREM LA MANO** 29
W. A. Mozart, *arranged by Ann Lindsay*

18 **19**   **9. GYMNOPÉDIE No. 1** 32
Erik Satie, *arranged by Ann Lindsay*

20 **21**   **10. IN THE HALL OF THE MOUNTAIN KING**
               from PEER GYNT SUITE No. 1 36
Edvard Grieg, *arranged by James Curnow*

22 **23**   **11. THE CARNIVAL OF VENICE** 40
Julius Benedict, *arranged by Mike Hannickel*

24 **25**   **12. THE BRITISH GRENADIERS** 44
Traditional, *arranged by James Curnow*

☐ **Solo with accompaniment**

■ **Accompaniment**

Ludwig van Beethoven
1. ODE TO JOY
Arr. **Timothy Johnson** (ASCAP)

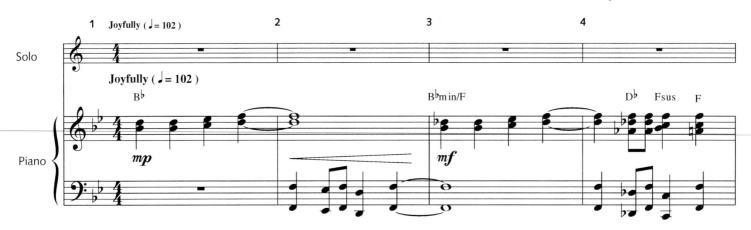

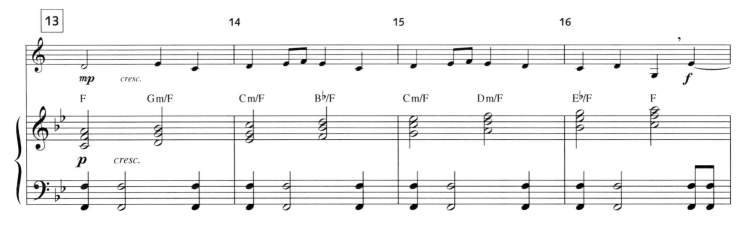

© 2005 by Curnow Music Press, Inc.

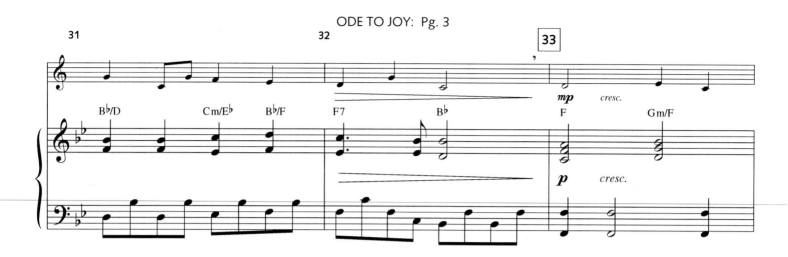

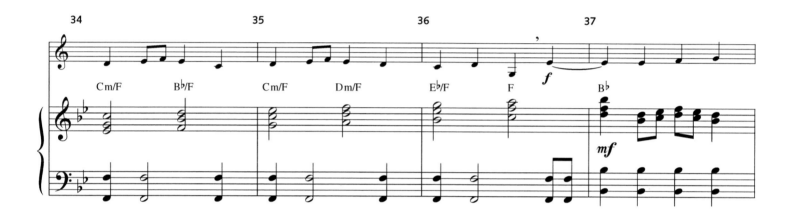

8

Franz Schubert
2. SANCTUS
Arr. **James Curnow** (ASCAP)

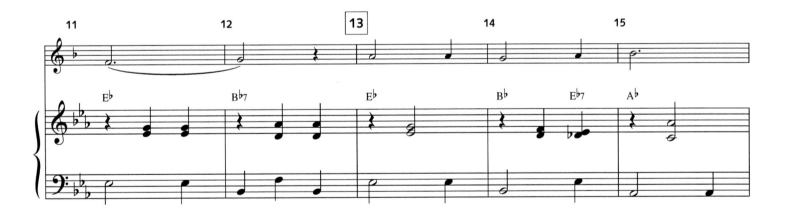

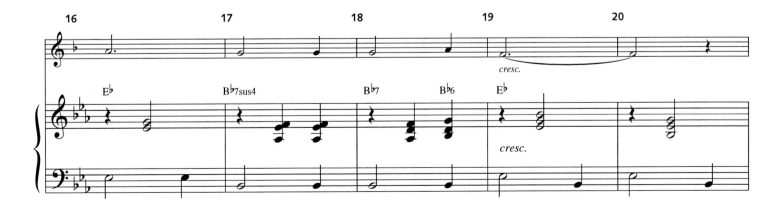

© 2005 by Curnow Music Press, Inc.

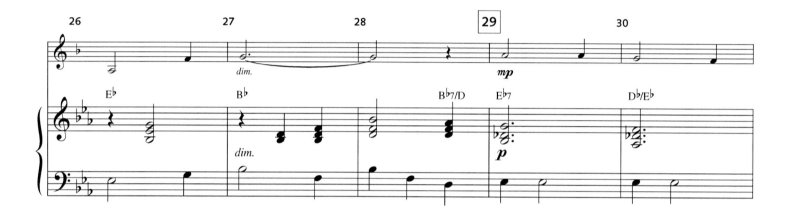

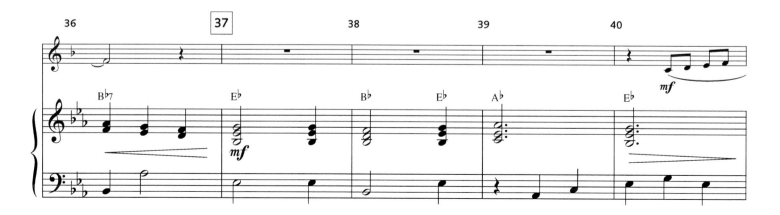

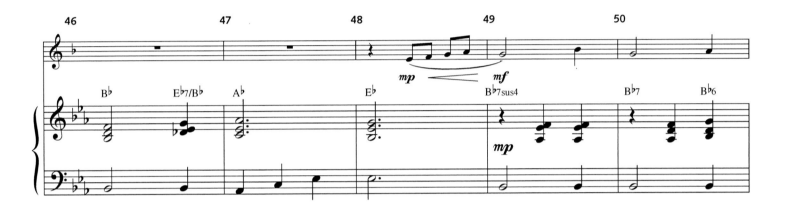

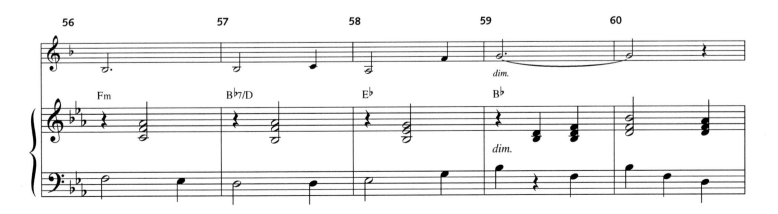

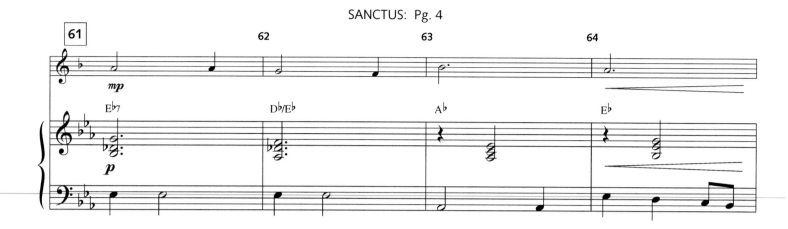

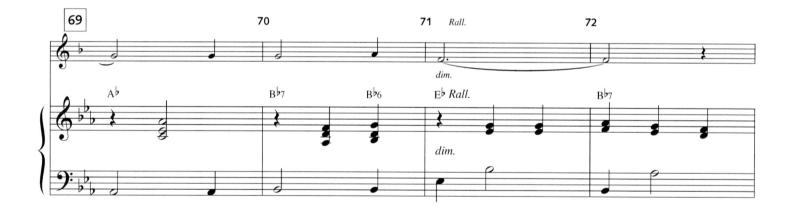

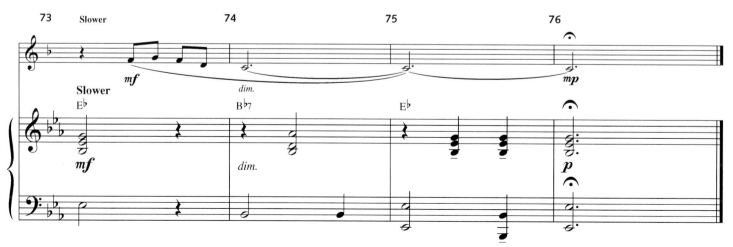

Victor Herbert
Fantasy On

3. DAGGER DANCE
from "NATOMA"

Arr. **Craig Alan** (ASCAP)

© 2005 by **Curnow Music Press, Inc.**

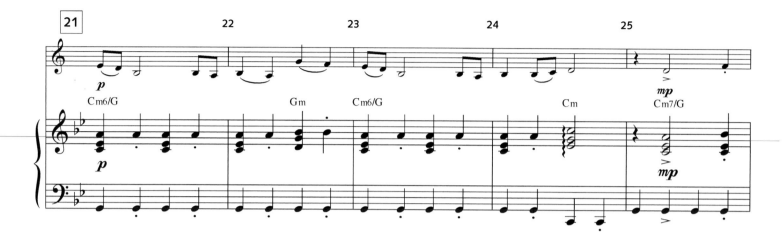

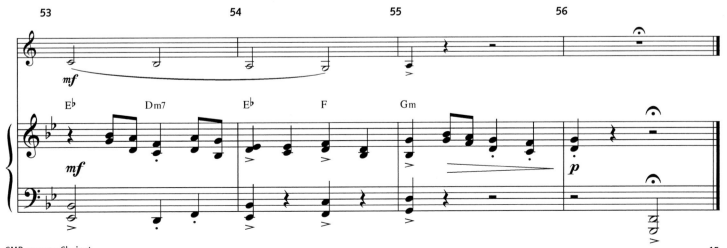

Johannes Brahms
4. FINALE FROM SYMPHONY #1

Arr. **Timothy Johnson** (ASCAP)

© 2005 by **Curnow Music Press, Inc.**

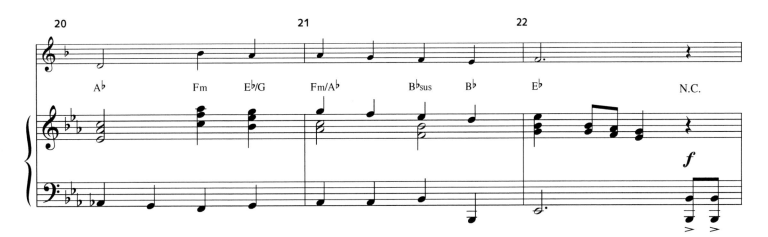

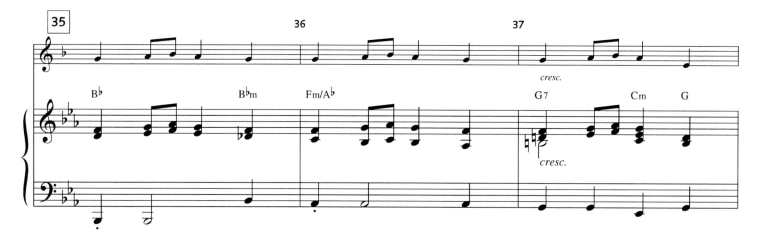

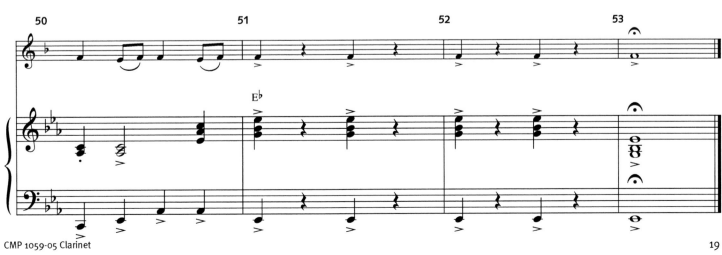

Frederic Chopin

5. FANTAISIE IMPROMPTU

Arr. **Ann Lindsay** (ASCAP)

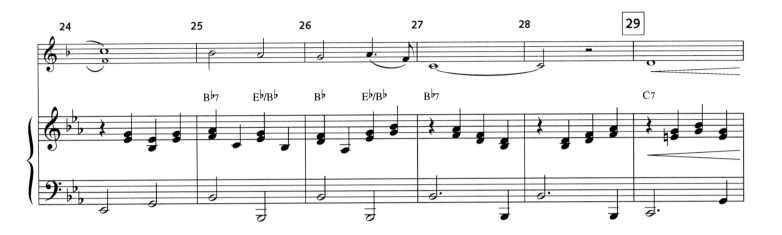

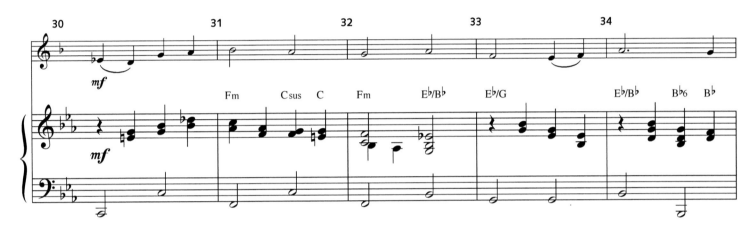

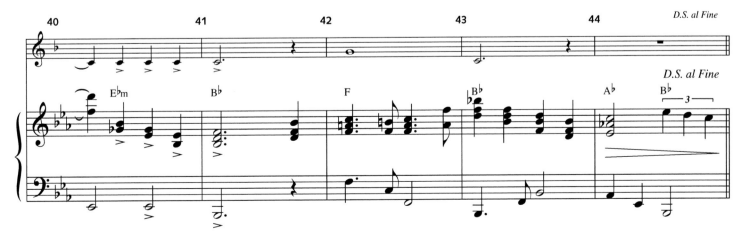

Johannes Brahms

6. HUNGARIAN DANCE NO.6

Arr. **Ann Lindsay** (ASCAP)

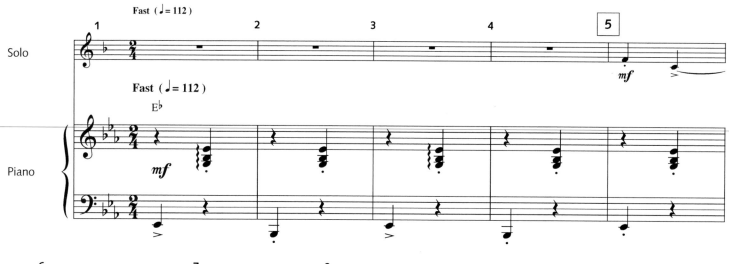

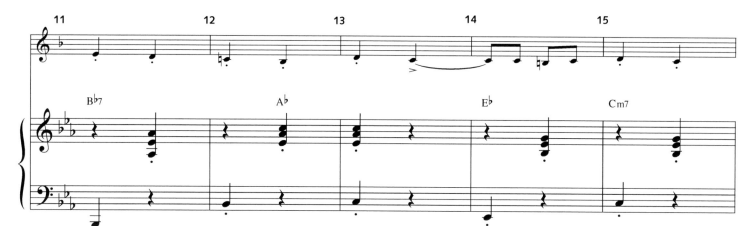

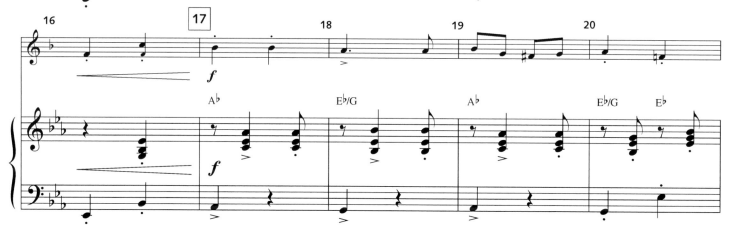

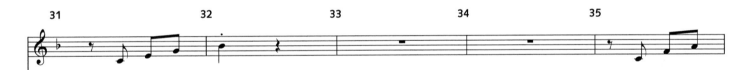

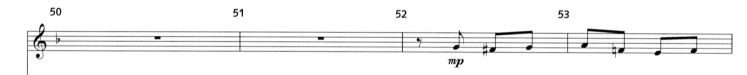

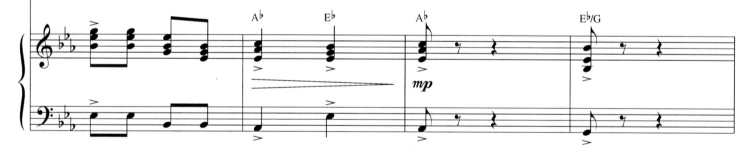

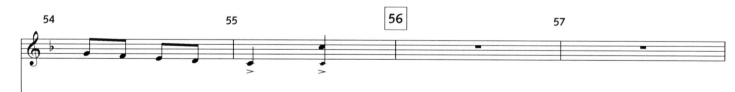

FOR THE YOUNG CLARINET PLAYER

FOREWORD

EASY CLASSICS FOR THE YOUNG CLARINET PLAYER is a compilation of solo/recital material from the great masters of musical composition that have been specifically arranged for the Beginner through Early Intermediate instrumental soloist. The soloist will find a wide variety of styles and varying levels of difficulty in this book.

This set includes the Piano accompaniment, the Solo part, and a professionally recorded CD that demonstrates each piece. Use these examples to help develop proper performance practices. There is also a recording of the accompaniment alone that can be used for performance (and rehearsal) when a live accompaniment is not available.

CURNOW® MUSIC

EXCLUSIVELY DISTRIBUTED BY

HAL•LEONARD® CORPORATION

7777 W. BLUEMOUND RD. P.O. BOX 13819 MILWAUKEE, WI 53213

CONTENTS

Track   page

1 **Tuning Note C**

2 **3** **1. ODE TO JOY** 3
Ludwig van Beethoven, arranged by Timothy Johnson

4 **5** **2. SANCTUS** 4
Franz Schubert, arranged by James Curnow

6 **7** **3. DAGGER DANCE from "NATOMA"** 5
Victor Herbert, arranged by Craig Alan

8 **9** **4. FINALE FROM SYMPHONY No. 1** 6
Johannes Brahms, arranged by Timothy Johnson

10 **11** **5. FANTAISIE IMPROMPTU** 7
Frederic Chopin, arranged by Ann Lindsay

12 **13** **6. HUNGARIAN DANCE No.6** 8
Johannes Brahms, arranged by Ann Lindsay

14 **15** **7. WALTZ** 9
Johannes Brahms, arranged by James Curnow

16 **17** **8. ANDANTE from LA CI DAREM LA MANO** 10
W. A. Mozart, arranged by Ann Lindsay

18 **19** **9. GYMNOPÉDIE No. 1** 11
Erik Satie, arranged by Ann Lindsay

20 **21** **10. IN THE HALL OF THE MOUNTAIN KING**
from PEER GYNT SUITE No. 1 12
Edvard Grieg, arranged by James Curnow

22 **23** **11. THE CARNIVAL OF VENICE** 14
Julius Benedict, arranged by Mike Hannickel

24 **25** **12. THE BRITISH GRENADIERS** 16
Traditional, arranged by James Curnow

☐ **Solo with accompaniment**

■ **Accompaniment**

Ludwig van Beethoven
1. ODE TO JOY
Arr. **Timothy Johnson** (ASCAP)

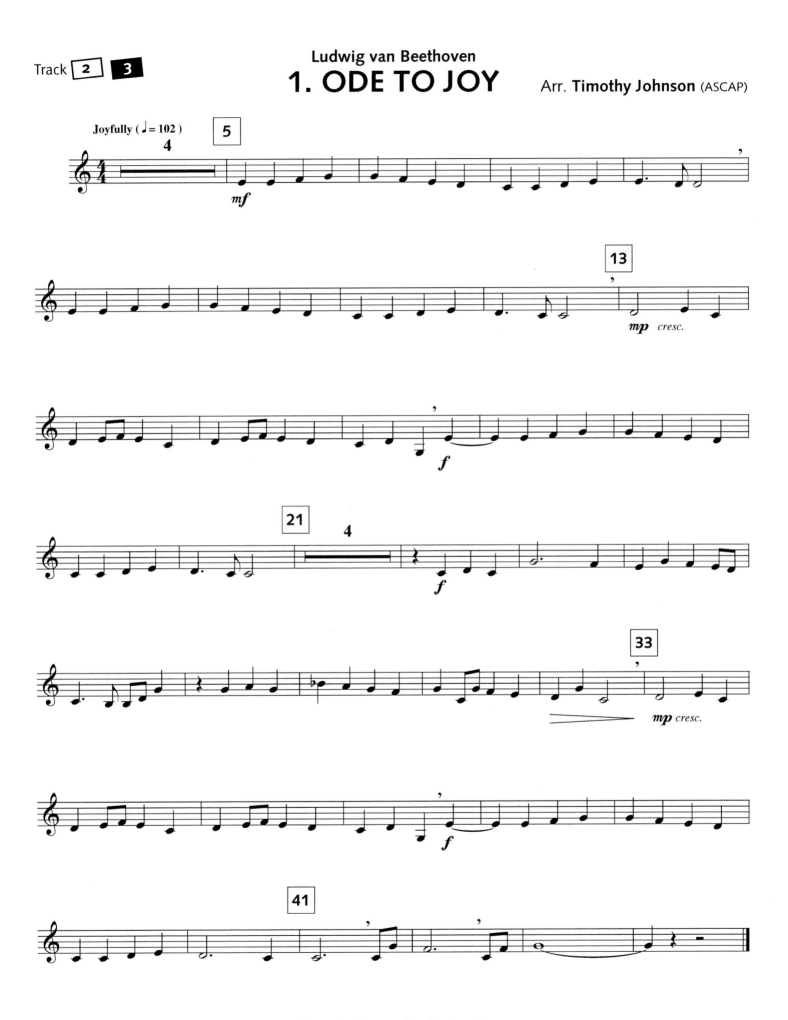

Franz Schubert
2. SANCTUS

Track 4 5

Arr. James Curnow (ASCAP)

Victor Herbert
Fantasy On

3. DAGGER DANCE
from "NATOMA"

Track **6** **7**

Arr. **Craig Alan** (ASCAP)

Johannes Brahms
4. FINALE FROM SYMPHONY #1

Arr. **Timothy Johnson** (ASCAP)

Frederic Chopin

5. FANTAISIE IMPROMPTU Arr. **Ann Lindsay** (ASCAP)

© 2005 by **Curnow Music Press, Inc.**

Johannes Brahms

6. HUNGARIAN DANCE NO.6

Arr. **Ann Lindsay** (ASCAP)

© 2005 by Curnow Music Press, Inc.

7. WALTZ

Johannes Brahms

Arr. **James Curnow** (ASCAP)

Track 14 15

Erik Satie
9. GYMNOPÉDIE No.1
Arr. **Ann Lindsay** (ASCAP)

Edvard Grieg

10. IN THE HALL OF THE MOUNTAIN KING

From Peer Gynt Suite #1

Arr. **James Curnow** (ASCAP)

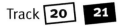

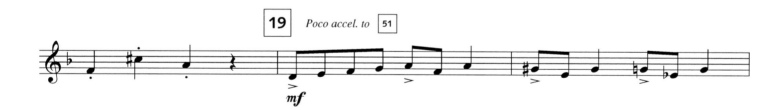

© 2005 by Curnow Music Press, Inc.

Julius Benedict
11. THE CARNIVAL OF VENICE

Arr. **Mike Hannickel** (ASCAP)

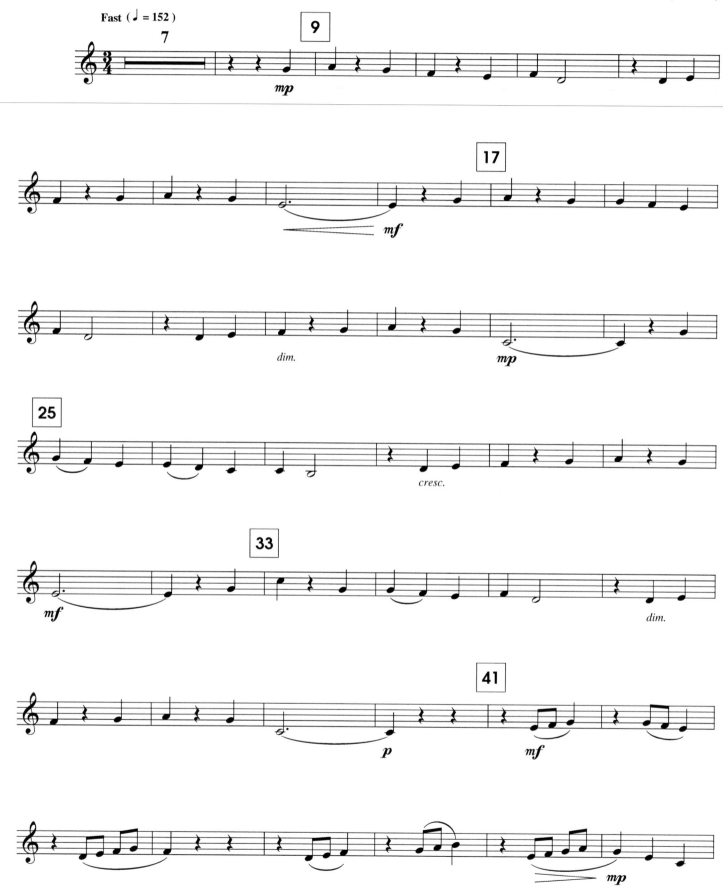

12. THE BRITISH GRENADIERS

Traditional
Arr. **James Curnow** (ASCAP)

CLASSICS FOR THE YOUNG CLARINET PLAYER

Music of the great masters: eight wonderful classics in a format that is appropriate for the young instrumentalist: from very easy up to early intermediate levels with a professionally recorded accompaniment CD. Excellent literature for concerts, contests, or home enjoyment. These solos can also be performed with a live band – they are also available as concert band arrangements.

Order Number   CMP 0544-01-400

CONCERT SOLOS FOR THE YOUNG CLARINET PLAYER

High quality solo pieces from very easy up to early intermediate levels with a professionally recorded demonstration/accompaniment CD. Features original compositions by some of today's finest composers for a total of twelve outstanding solos in a wide variety of musical styles. Excellent literature for concerts, contests, church, or home enjoyment. Piano accompaniment included.

Order Number   CMP 1047-05-400

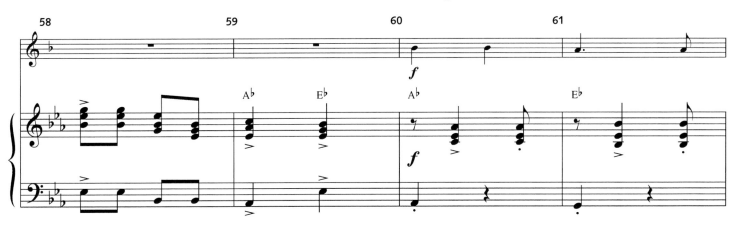

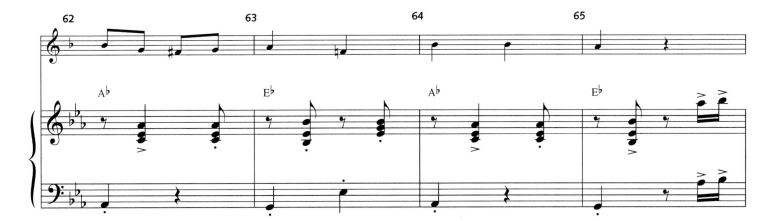

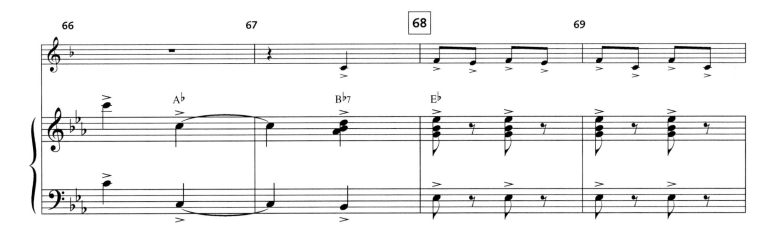

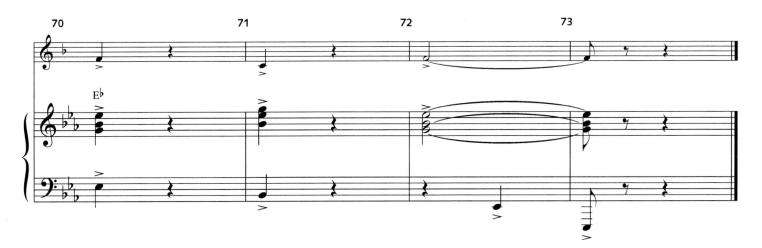

7. WALTZ

Track 14 15

Arr. **James Curnow** (ASCAP)

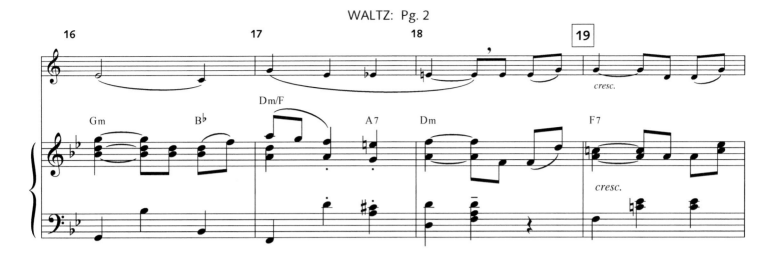

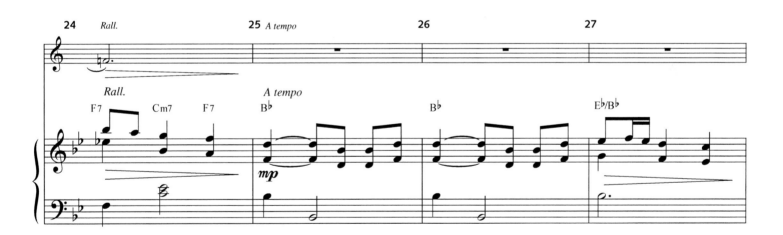

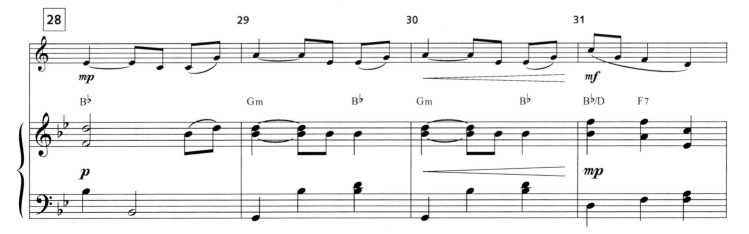

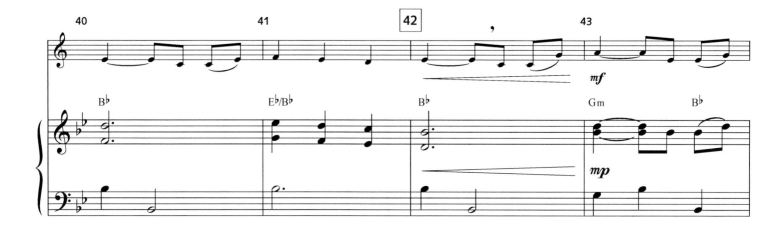

W. A. Mozart
8. ANDANTE
from LA CI DAREM LA MANO

From Don Giovanni

Arr. **Ann Lindsay** (ASCAP)

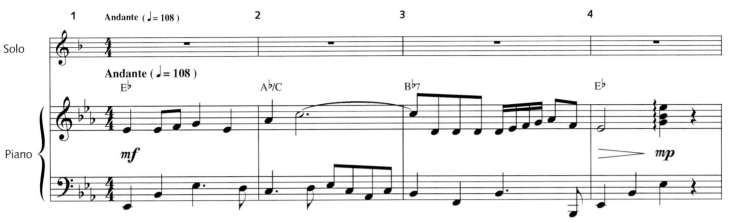

© 2005 by **Curnow Music Press, Inc.**

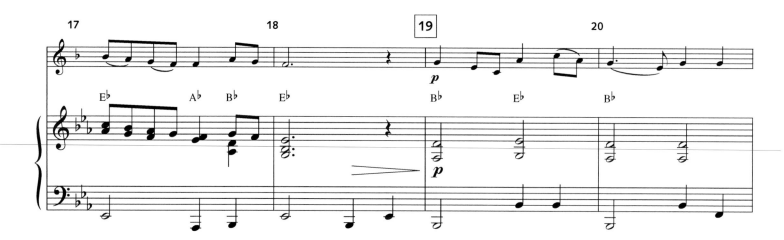

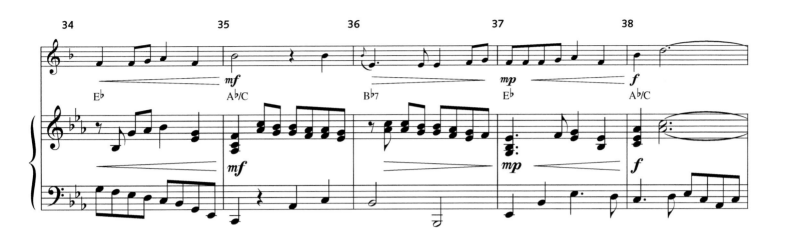

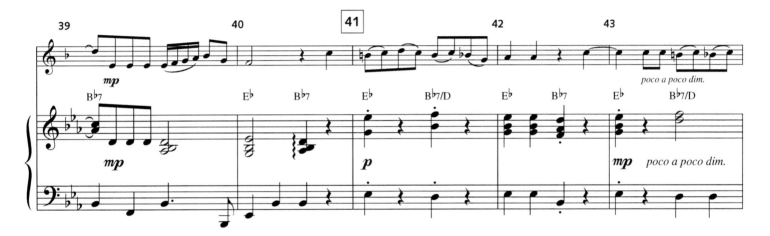

Erik Satie

9. GYMNOPÉDIE No.1

Arr. **Ann Lindsay** (ASCAP)

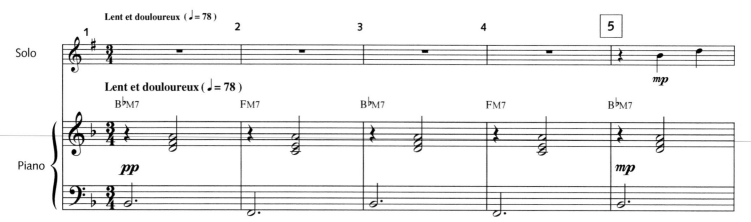

Pedal harmonically throughout

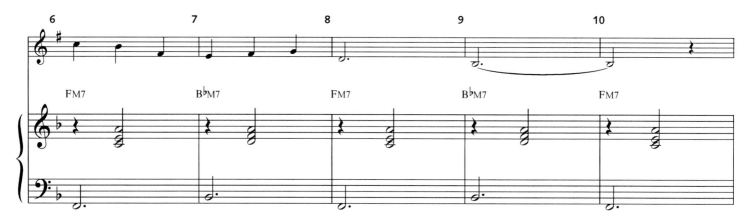

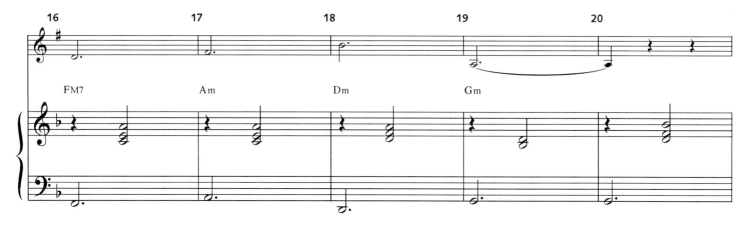

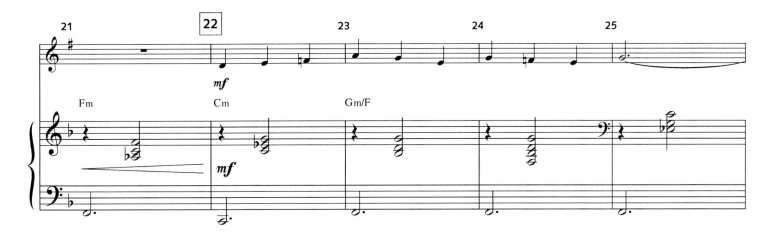

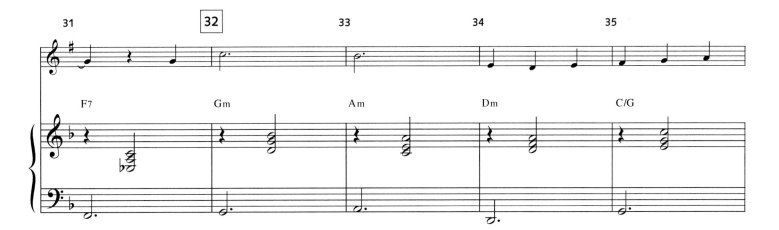

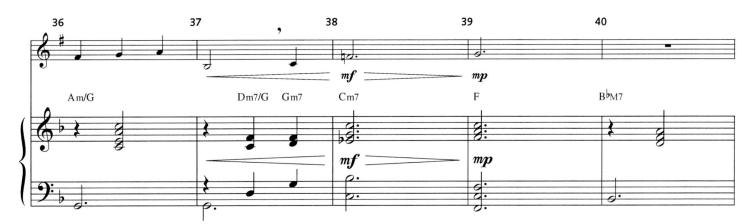

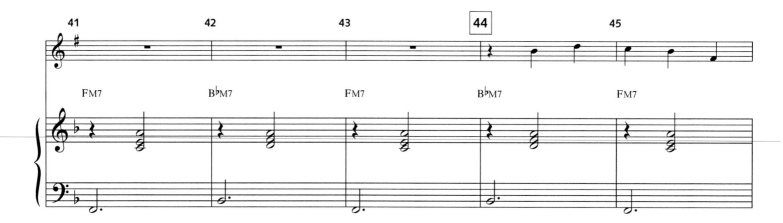

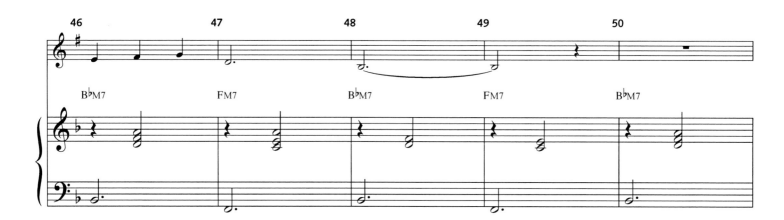

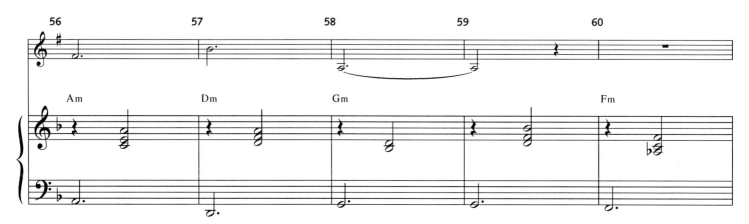

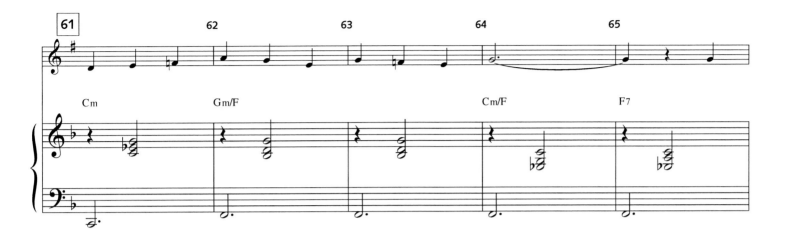

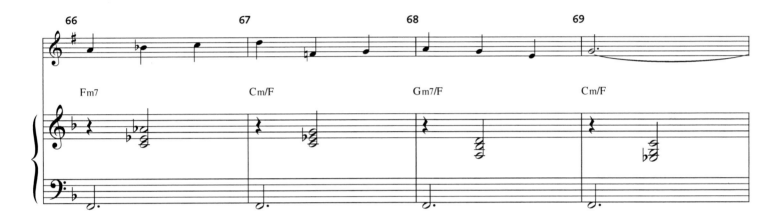

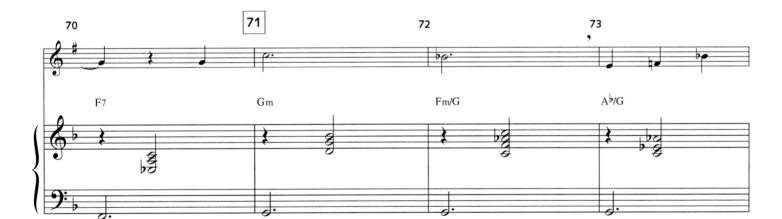

Edvard Grieg
10. IN THE HALL OF THE MOUNTAIN KING
From Peer Gynt Suite #1
Arr. **James Curnow** (ASCAP)

© 2005 by **Curnow Music Press, Inc.**

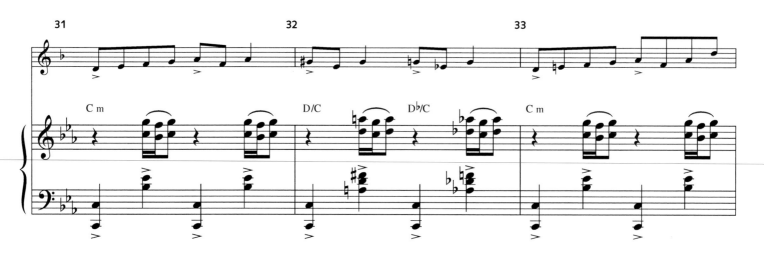

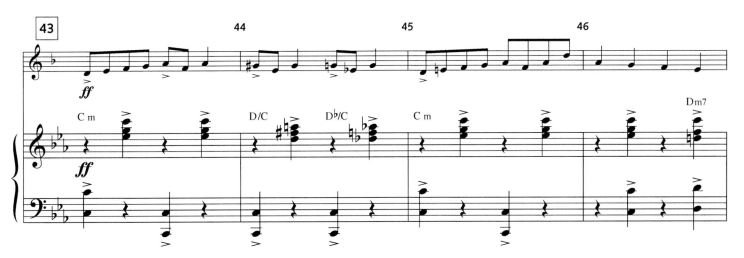

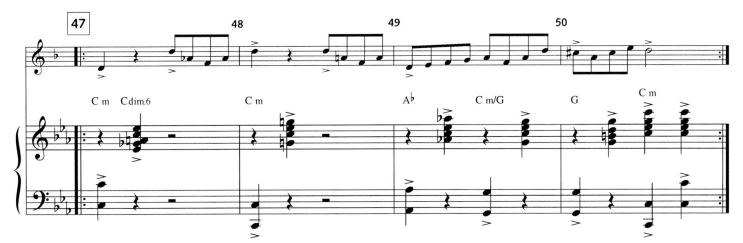

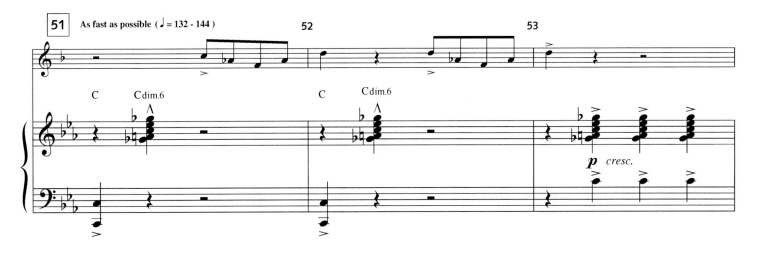

Julius Benedict

11. THE CARNIVAL OF VENICE

Arr. **Mike Hannickel** (ASCAP)

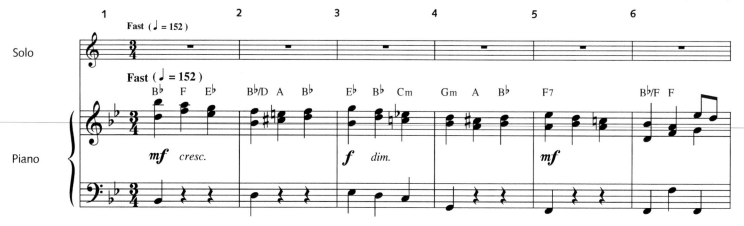

40

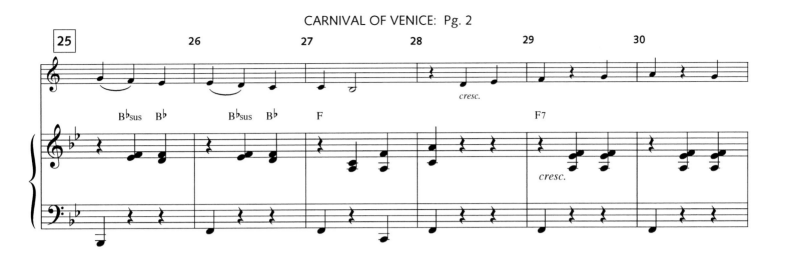

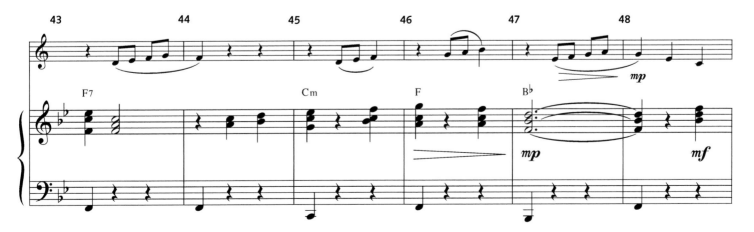

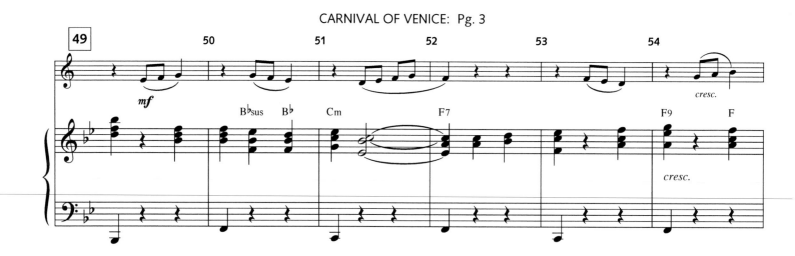

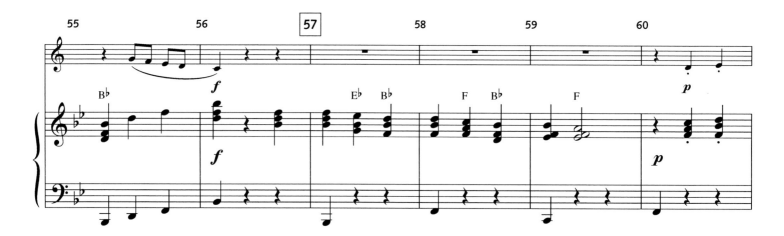

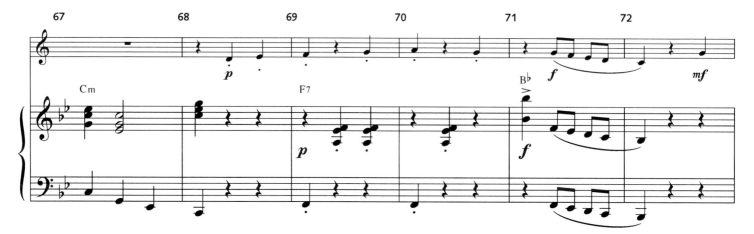

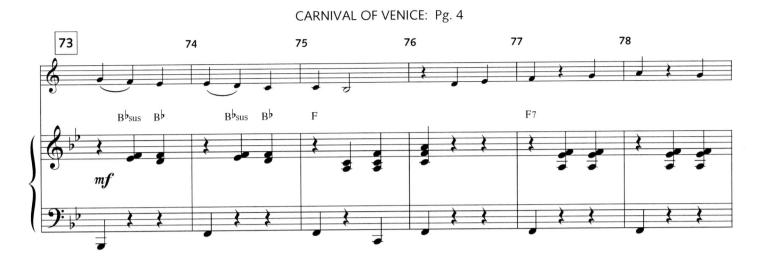

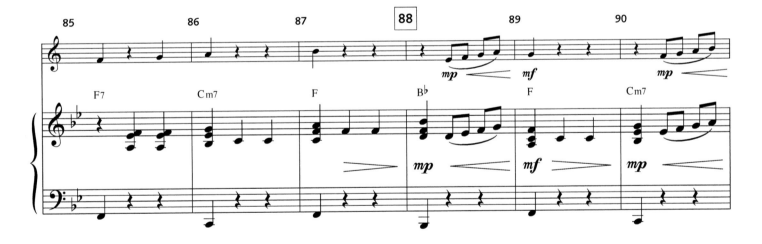

12. THE BRITISH GRENADIERS

Traditional
Arr. **James Curnow** (ASCAP)

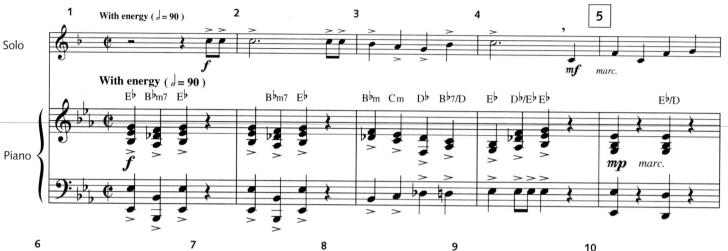

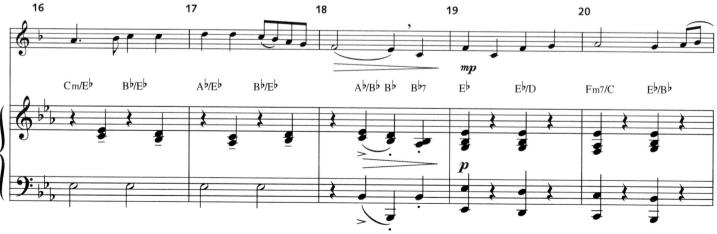

© 2005 by **Curnow Music Press, Inc.**

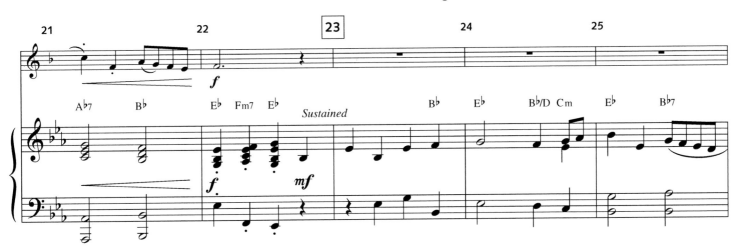

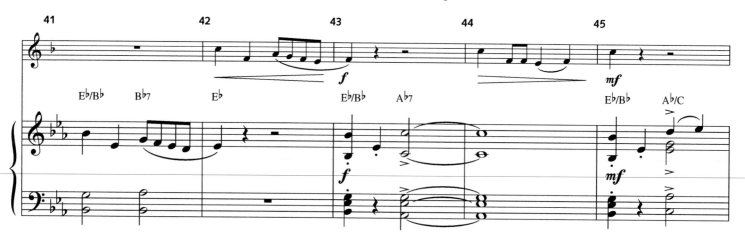

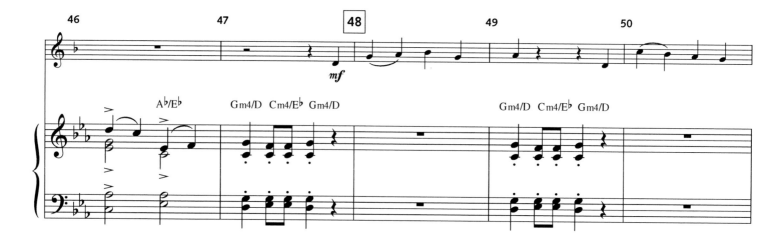

CLASSICS FOR THE YOUNG CLARINET PLAYER

Music of the great masters: eight wonderful classics in a format that is appropriate for the young instrumentalist: from very easy up to early intermediate levels with a professionally recorded accompaniment CD. Excellent literature for concerts, contests, or home enjoyment. These solos can also be performed with a live band – they are also available as concert band arrangements.

Order Number   CMP 0544-01-400

CONCERT SOLOS FOR THE YOUNG CLARINET PLAYER

High quality solo pieces from very easy up to early intermediate levels with a professionally recorded demonstration/accompaniment CD. Features original compositions by some of today's finest composers for a total of twelve outstanding solos in a wide variety of musical styles. Excellent literature for concerts, contests, church, or home enjoyment. Piano accompaniment included.

Order Number   CMP 1047-05-400